Understanding a Bipolar Child

Understanding a Bipolar Child

TARA NICOLE SCOTT BRUNSON

Illustrations by Brian Wade Scott

iUniverse, Inc.
Bloomington

UNDERSTANDING A BIPOLAR CHILD

iUniverse books may be ordered through booksellers or by contacting:

iUniverse
1663 Liberty Drive
Bloomington, IN 47403
www.iuniverse.com
1-800-Authors (1-800-288-4677)

ISBN: 978-1-4620-6914-9 (sc)
ISBN: 978-1-4620-6916-3 (hc)
ISBN: 978-1-4620-6915-6 (ebk)

Printed in the United States of America

iUniverse rev. date: 11/16/2011

This book is dedicated to my son Jay—I would not be the person I am today without you—thank you, my love; to my wonderful family, for all your support and unconditional love; and to all the people who are struggling with ADHD, bipolar disorder, or both.

Introduction

It's the hardest thing in the world to see your child in pain, whether it's your two-year-old who has an owie or a ten-year-old, who has just experienced a broken heart for the first time. Sometimes, no one can find what ails your child from within. Parents often reach their wits' end trying to spare their child from his or her pains; some give up everything to find a remedy. I wanted to tell my story to help others learn to cope with child diagnosed with ADHD or bipolar disorder.

Chapter 1

Stories of a Bipolar Child

I was awakened in the middle of the night by a loud thud, followed by a horrifying cry. It was my baby! My little son Jay started climbing at a very early age; he climbed on everything within his reach. Even before he could crawl, he could climb. Initially it made me very nervous, especially his early endeavors.

Now, that anxiety had jolted me awake. Jay, a little scamp of just nine months, had crept out of his crib and made his way over to the dresser to begin his climb. I could imagine how he had climbed slowly, with wobbling steps, until the dresser suddenly toppled over his little body. When the dresser gave a huge bang, I sprang out of my bed, threw the dresser off my baby, and pulled him into my arms. I embraced him for a few moments and then examined him for any bruises on his tender body. Fortunately, I saw no visible signs of injuries; in my trauma from the incident, it appeared I was the only casualty.

Jay could swim before he could walk. Water is very dangerous for small children, especially those as curious as Jay. Understanding the importance of water safety is crucial, so I worked with him every day to teach him how to swim. When we would go out to the community pool, people would stare, dumbfounded, at my tiny son swimming like a fish. Jay could go across any part of the pool. He would go underwater and pretend to drown until he came up gasping for breath; this was just a trick to fool people.

Jay was about fifteen months old when Kevin, Jay's grandmother Corrine new boyfriend, decided he wanted to show his girlfriend what a loving and caring person he was. He told

Corrine, that he would take Jay on his errands with him. The first stop would be the bank.

Kevin hadn't realized Jay wasn't wearing a diaper, only underwear (he was being potty trained). While Kevin talked to the teller, disputing an unfair overdraft charge, Kevin became increasingly frustrated, but still was holding Jay's hand. Jay started getting antsy, so Kevin released his hand and saw Jay go into a small playhouse set up to occupy children while their parents took care of business in the bank.

Kevin then shouted to the teller, "I want to speak to your superior!" When the supervisor had arrived, Jay was still nowhere in sight. Kevin kept arguing with the bank manager until he started smelling a foul odor. Kevin started to look around for the smell, curious about what it could be. He then saw Jay out of the corner of his eye, coming around the corner of the bank tellers' station with his pants in one hand and nothing covering his bottom—or any other part of his body. Aside from the poop covering him from head to toe, Jay was completely naked.

Jay had smeared poop all over the walls and floors of the bank, and everyone around was looking at Jay with horror. Just to get Kevin out of the bank, the manager told him, "All right, sir, we will refund the charges. Whatever you want."

Kevin went over to Jay and took him by the hand.

"Damn right you will," Kevin told the bank teller and stomped out of the bank.

By the time Jay was about a year and a half old, it was not unusual for me to wake up at any hour of the night to find eggs dumped all over the floor of the kitchen or even see the entire refrigerator emptied onto the living-room floor. Through the eyes of a toddler, eggs have an uncanny resemblance to baseballs. Jay would take an egg from the refrigerator just to throw it against the wall while yelling "Ball, ball!"

I guess I should be thankful that he was taken up with baseball. I shudder to think what my house would have looked like if Jay had been a WWF wrestling fan instead!

Even so, I probably should have made a practice of boiling all those eggs *before* I put them in the refrigerator!

When Jay was just under two years old, he had awoken during the middle of the night. Unlike many children, Jay always wanted to solve problems on his own. For instance, if he felt hungry, he would neither wake me nor his grandmother; instead, he would invade the kitchen and try to conquer the pantry and the cupboards until he found something that caught his eye.

That morning, Jay climbed into the cupboards and spotted a bright-red box with a picture of a pancake on it. He stretched out his little arm into the rear of the pantry for the box of pancake mix. As syrup is always the best part of pancakes, Jay made sure to get his little fingers around both the box and the bottle before pulling them out of the pantry.

Jay, now back on his two little feet, walked out of the kitchen, through the living room, and into the bedroom while holding both items upside down, leaving a sticky, gooey trail behind him. He climbed onto the bed with the box of pancake mix and the half-empty syrup bottle.

Out of excitement, as if he'd won a million dollars from the lottery, he jumped up and down repeatedly on the bed, his loud shrieks of excitement drumming into his grandmother's ears: "Grandma, Grandma, wake up! I'm hungry. I want pancakes!" Innocently, he emptied the leftovers of the dry pancake mix and the syrup onto the head of his grandmother.

Long ago, we had a cat, and when our cat was only about six months old, we realized she was pregnant. One night Jay was playing with the cat, running around and chasing her. I kept telling him to stop, but before I knew it, her water broke. The cat had trouble delivering the kittens, but while on the phone with the vet, I was able to help the cat bring her babies into the world.

A few weeks after the kittens were born, Jay became determined to play with them. He would sneak each out of their box one at a time. But Jay was much rougher with them than he meant to be. I tried to sit him down and explain to him that the new kittens were just babies, and that we had to be nice and gentle to babies. But one day I was doing laundry and found one of the little kittens in the dryer. Jay told me he had wanted the kitten to go for a ride. Jay still remembers the little kittens and has vaguely unpleasant memories about them but doesn't remember what exactly what happened. At that time, Jay was barely two years old. He loved those kittens, and he didn't realize that what he was doing would hurt them.

Jay learned very early how to open the front door, so I installed a flip lock onto the door. But when Jay managed to push his high chair from the dining room up against the front door in the living room, he knew he had outsmarted me. Jay could undo the knob lock and then climb the chair to reach the flip lock. Once Jay was able to get the door unlocked, he would wander off to the playgrounds.

The front door was not Jay's only route of escape. We lived in a small apartment, and the backyard was a concrete patio enclosed by a wooden fence. Jay enjoyed playing outside, and I felt he was safe to play alone inside our confined patio if I were doing chores in the home, like putting away laundry or cooking. Unfortunately I couldn't see him from every room, but I was close enough to hear him, which I thought was enough. But one sunny day, while I was cooking dinner and Jay was playing out back, I got a knock at the door. It was a couple of kids about eight years old telling me that my baby was on the basketball court.

I ran out the door. The basketball court was not far away—thankfully he didn't have to cross any streets to get there—but the idea that he was able to get out of the yard in just a matter of minutes was shocking and terrifying to me.

Once I had brought my baby back home, I told him how scary it had been for Mommy to know where he was and that he could have gotten hurt. I told him to never take off like that again.

When I went into the backyard, I discovered how he had in fact been able to vanish from the patio. It had not been a vanishing act at all; he had used the same technique that he had used to open the front door. Jay had stacked all his toys up against the fence and climbed up each toy: a rocking horse, a chair, even a large bouncy ball. Once he had climbed high enough, he had thrown his body over the fence. I assume Jay had seen children playing basketball and wanted to join them.

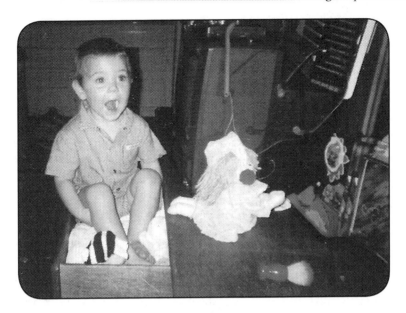

I walked into the bedroom and caught Jay inside the dresser drawer.

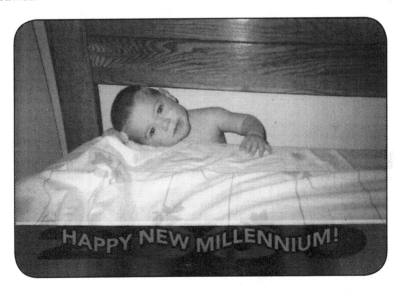

As a young child, Jay hid behind and underneath everything he could. This is a picture of Jay stuck behind my headboard.

I was working for a company installing coupons on the shelves in supermarkets. Needless to say, I had boxes of coupons. Like many other two-year-old children, Jay was busy learning to use the potty. One evening, while Jay was sitting on the potty, the phone rang. As I ran to answer it, I heard a knock at the door at the same time. I picked up the receiver and walked to the door with it without answering the call.

A stocky man stood at the door, waiting to deliver a pizza. But my brother, who had ordered it, was not at home at the moment. Somehow the phone's wire got wrapped around the man's leg, which I did not notice. As I walked back into the bedroom, I heard something falling down with a great thud. I also found myself walking into what felt like a rushing stream. Jay had clogged the toilet with diapers and packets of coupon booklets. Water was spraying out of the toilet. Before I could do anything, something pulled me back, and I fell backward onto the stocky man, who was lying on the ground!

When Jay was little, around two, I would take showers with him. One day, when I finished showering, I got out and wrapped my robe around myself. I then extended my arm for Jay. As he stood up, he began to slip. Immediately, he grabbed and held the glass shower door, regrettably, which wasn't sturdy enough to hold even his diminutive body weight. Just as he grabbed the shower knob, the door toppled down on top of his little body. I thank God that he was within my reach. I clutched him with every fiber of my mortal being and ripped his tiny body out of the tub. Without delay, I called my aunt, who is chief nurse of her hospital. She quickly drove over. When evaluating Jay's cuts, we realized that he had only suffered minor injuries, and only then from the waist down. Fortunately they were trifling cuts. When I attempted to clean up the mess in the shower, I didn't even know where to start. At first glance, one might think it was full of water, but a closer look would bring a startling realization: it was full of glass.

When I started realizing Jay was unlike other two year old kids I took him to several doctors to analyze his behaviors. Upon walking in the door of the doctor's office, I found it obvious that they saw mostly children. Two of the four walls of the waiting room were painted a sky blue with puffy white clouds sporadically placed, as if they were flowing across the walls. On the other two walls were grass and flowers, along with animals. The walls with the animals had a cartoonish feel.

The waiting room was set up to keep children occupied while waiting to be seen. A coloring table was in one corner and a television in the other, showing cartoons. Sitting in the waiting room, Jay became fascinated with a large fish tank in the middle of the room. The fish were fluorescent—so bright and colorful.

After we had waited about ten minutes, the doctor was ready to see us. However, once the doctor had evaluated Jay and asked me a series of questions, she said she couldn't pinpoint what was wrong with him. Several days prior, I had read an article about autism and noticed that he showed signs of it. When I asked the doctor about this, she said he was absolutely not autistic and referred me to a behavioral specialist.

After leaving the doctor's office, I buckled Jay into his car seat and started to prepare to leave. But when I sat down in the driver's seat, I started crying uncontrollably.

With force in my voice, I began yelling at myself. "Why is my baby unlike all the other kids? Did I somehow cause this? It is my fault! I must have done something wrong! Am I terrible mother? Of course I'm an awful mom. If I were a good mom, he would not behave so badly."

After a couple of minutes, I had exhausted myself, and my whole body went limp. I sat quietly in the car for a few moments, tears rolling down my face, before driving us home.

I got a call a few days later from the behavioral specialist that Jay's doctor had referred us to. The specialist asked me questions about my child: What types of behaviors was he experiencing? Did he feel pain or empathy? Did our family have a history of any mental disorders? I was told I needed to bring him in to have him assessed in order to find a medication that would work for him.

When I told the man on the phone I was not putting my two-year-old baby on medications, he told me, "If you're not even willing to consider medications, don't bother coming in"—and then he hung up on me. When I put the phone down, I was in shock. How dare he? I just wanted answers, and this doctor was not even willing to meet with us because I did not want to put my baby on medications that could possibly harm his little body. I felt as if I had hit a roadblock yet again.

housing. Base housing is very safe, to say the least: a full military ID check is mandatory for everyone there.

While Jay was outdoors playing, I would often do a quick peekaboo to make sure he was fine. To my surprise, this particular day, I looked out the window to find Jay standing by the trash cans at the curb. The garbage truck was coming down the street to take the weekly garbage away. To my horror, when the truck was picking up trash, Jay got hold of the big metal arm of the trash truck and went up with it. But the saving grace was that when the truck was about to empty the trash, Jay jumped like a frog and landed safely on the ground.

One day, Jay and his grandmother Corrine went to a grocery store, with Jay being his usual self, filling the shopping cart with whatever his short little hands could reach. Once Jay had loaded all the frozen food that he desired into the cart, he suddenly went to the end of the aisle to snatch a cereal box by its cap.

The box he seized had stood at the center of a large display of boxes, and the entire thing fell with a crashing sound; even the box Jay had wanted went down with the rest of the mess.

A nearby woman had witnessed Jay's actions. In a flash, she approached Jay's grandmother to shower her with complaints, thundering, "You need to do something about this kid, as he's wild and running amok!"

His grandmother responded calmly, "You need to mind your own business. No one speaks about my grandson like that.

When Jay was three years old, Jay, my mom, and I went to the local nail salon. Because Jay wasn't getting a pedicure. While my mom and I had our toes done, Jay sat quietly, playing. When the door of the salon swung open, Jay looked up to watch a woman walk in. The woman was about five foot four and around 250 pounds, wearing an oversize t-shirt.

Without saying a word, Jay jumped up, ran to her, lifted her shirt up, and gave her raspberries on her bear stomach.

In Jay's mind, this behavior was appropriate; at home, we played the raspberry game quite often, and he loved it. Jay would lie on the floor, and I would sit on my knees and ask him a series of questions:

Do you like strawberries?
Do you like blueberries?
Do you like blackberries?
Do you like boysenberries?
How about *raspberries*?
Then I would blow raspberries on his tummy.

But his doing this to this potbellied woman was totally unexpected and extremely embarrassing as she turned around to storm out of the nail shop.

One day, when Jay was about five years old, he was outside playing with the neighborhood kids from across the street. We lived in a two-story home on a cul-de-sac in the middle of base

Jay innocently ran to his grandmother, asking, "What went wrong, Grandma? Why is she so upset?"

Jay has always been the sweetest, kindest, and most generous person I have ever met. He used to think that to be someone's friend, he had to give that person something every time he see him or her. He would often sit in his room, wrapping his own toys in wrapping paper to give to his friends. His dad and I have explained to him that true friends don't expect anything other than his friendship. Today, he understands he doesn't have to give all his things away, but he enjoys seeing how happy it makes others to receive gifts, and that's why he continues to do it.

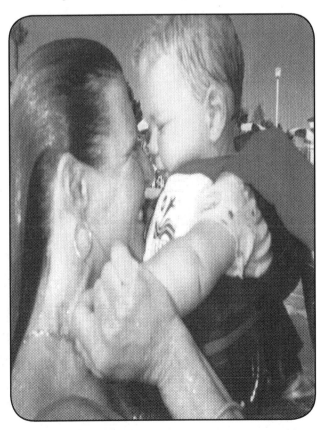

Jay has always been my little cuddle bug. I love it when he curls up with me and we watch a movie or read a book together. Since his medications have been helping him, I can reflect on the good times we share and not spend all my time being so angry about his behavior all the time. When his meltdowns were constant, I put so much energy into being upset over everything. Research shows that running your hand over a child's arm can soothe a child having a meltdown, but quite honestly, there have been times when I could not even touch him because I was so upset. I am so thankful we are able to truly enjoy one another again.

I had learned that using sign language (ASL) could help parents communicate with their special-needs children. I chose to major in nursing and minor in American Sign Language so that I could teach my son sign language. Eventually we both became fluent. I have found that signing really does help us communicate better, especially during meltdowns and while in public. Instead of yelling, I use my hands, and he can understand just what I want him to do. I have found that even in the middle of a meltdown, if I sing to Jay that he needs to settle down, he calms down more quickly because he is paying attention to me rather than having a yelling match. Studies show that singing with autistic kids helps bridge communication.

I will never forget the day we moved out of our house in northern California. As the movers loaded the last bit of our furniture into the truck, my husband and I walked around upstairs, double-checking each room for anything left behind. Jay, then about five years old, was downstairs in the garage. When I walked into the garage, I caught Jay literally red-handed, or was it another color? With a bottle of spray paint. He had painted all the shelving and the floor—oh, yes, let's not forget the entire garage door. This was also the day I found out that Magic Erasers don't remove spray paint from metal.

I spent the entire night trying to get rid of any evidence of what Jay had done. It's a good thing my neighbor just happened to have a can of paint to match the shelving, but I should have remembered to give the can of paint back before the final inspection the next morning.

Chapter 2

Medication and School

As time went on, my husband and I started to realize that we would have to consider medications to help Jay get control over his own actions. One of my main concerns was that Jay didn't stop to think before he acted; if medications calmed him down enough to help him stop and look before running out into the street, I would at least consider medication for my child's safety.

One day my husband and I sat down to figure out the best thing to do for all of us. My husband was completely against medicating our child from the start, but seeing how unhappy my baby was in his own skin, I wanted to stay open to other options. In the past we had tried limiting him to only certain foods and then bringing the other foods back into his diet one by one. I had been told that a food allergy to a specific ingredient, such as gluten, could be the culprit of his wild behaviors. Quickly we found out that was not the problem. I also tried to stimulate him with coffee. The story goes that if a child who has ADD is given coffee, it will have the opposite effect on him that it would on someone without ADD. I drink coffee in the morning. The caffeine gives me energy, but I reasoned that if Jay drank coffee, it should calm him down. But we quickly found this didn't work for him, either.

My talk with my husband about medications ended with what I thought to be a fair compromise: we would wait until Jay was at least six years old and in first grade. This way we could also get several opinions from teachers. A teacher would see Jay differently than we did at home, and she would also have experience of knowing what behavior were acceptable and not acceptable for a child his age.

Knowing your family's psychiatric history is important for the doctor to be able to start to diagnose the disorder. Bipolar disorder runs in my family. My mom was diagnosed with Bipolar disorder when she was 17 years old, as did her mom, and Jay was diagnosed at 10 years old.

Before administering a new medication to your child, it is always necessary to be aware of any side effects. I always do as much research as possible on the medication that is recommended for my child. Several times, my son has told me that he felt as if his heart were going to beat out of his chest. I would take his blood pressure and pulse throughout the day as well during the night, while he was sleeping, just to be safe. I am one who believes medication should only be taken when it is truly necessary, because risk is always involved. Especially in children, we cannot be sure how the body will react to a substance.

When Jay started kindergarten, his teacher immediately wanted him to wait another year before starting school due to his immaturity. Although Jay hadn't attended a preschool, I felt it was important for him to go ahead and stay in school. During the middle of first grade, we tried adding medications, and they seemed to help just a little as far as helping him stay focused. When those medications no longer worked, we went on to try others, and this turned into a vicious cycle.

Jay struggled through each grade and was not held back, thanks to No Child Left Behind. When Jay was in third grade, his meltdowns became unalterable for the school, and they put him on half days.

They said, "He's normal in the mornings, but you'll have to pick him up around lunchtime." I found this unfair to my child, as he was missing out on the entire afternoon studies and was going to fall way behind the rest of his classmates. Once he had been labeled with a disorder, the school called me in anytime he sneezed. I felt his medications were no longer working, and I was becoming more frustrated, having tried more than fifteen medications by this point of time. Some of them even affected his kidneys and liver. This is when I decided to have him weaned off all the medications he was on to see if he did better without having all those chemicals in his system.

But I made the mistake of telling the school what I was up to, and they informed me that if I didn't put him back onto his medications, he would not be allowed back into the school.

The next step was to start Jay on an IEP.

An IEP (individualized education plan) is a written document; it is an essential tool in getting your child all the educational resources available. The first step would be to tell your child's teacher you are considering an IEP and would like a meeting. It is important to walk into the meeting strong and confident, ready to fight for your child. The IEP meeting is usually held twice a year: once at the start of the school year and again toward the end of the school year. The meeting often involves the child's teacher, counselor, principal, and at times the school nurse, depending on the child's special needs. The benefit of an IEP is the establishment of goals for the child to achieve before the next meeting. If the child has trouble in math, the IEP can state that the child will be pulled out of the classroom during math time for one-on-one mathematical help; the same goes for any subject. When my son was in third grade, he had trouble sitting still in his chair, so in his IEP we wrote that when he felt an excessive amount of energy, he could get up out of his chair, walk out of the classroom, take a lap around the building, and then return quietly to his seat.

Chapter 3

Journal Entries

When my son was around nine years old, I decided to start a journal. The journal started off as a way of keeping track of his behaviors. It is important to chart behaviors from day to day as a reference for Jay's doctors. The doctors appreciate that I am able to remember in detail each episode, along with the date and time. This is especially helpful when he is starting a new medication, allowing the doctor to decipher whether it is working. Even when Jay spends the night at his grandparents' houses, I always ask them to keep a daily log. It is a good idea to keep track of a child's behaviors and monitor whether they are experiencing similar behaviors at the same time of day, regardless of where they are.

I found that if I kept the journal in my purse, I was more apt to remember to write in it. The amount of information on each page doesn't have to be more then a few sentences; each entry will be a reminder of your child's actions from one day to the next. As a mother of four, I take advantage when I am parked in front of my kid's school, waiting for the bell to ring, or in a long line at the post office. During those brief breaks, I jot down a few key points about my son's day. I will share several journal entries to give an example of how simple each can be.

July 3, 2009

Jay actually got up all by himself this morning for summer school at about 6:15 a.m. We played a game of Phase 10 before we had to leave, but he was more interested in the television than our card game. Jay told me he was tired just before he got on the bus. When Jay got home from school at about 1:00 p.m., he behaved until he tried to unlock the door. The door was stuck, and I asked Jay repeatedly to stop forcing the key in the door, but he refused. He broke the key in the lock!

About an hour later, we went to Jay's therapist, and Jay could not sit still in his office. He ran out of the building and into the grocery store adjacent to the therapist's office "to use the bathroom." He also ran off to the car twice. When we returned home, Jay took off to the park without asking, and it took me twenty-five minutes to get him back home. Once Jay was home, he refused to take a bath or go to bed. I am so frustrated!

It's now 11:30 p.m., and Jay got Zack up out of bed, and they are both running around like chickens with their heads cut off.

Midnight: they are finally asleep!

August 8, 2009

Jay was awoken at 8:30 a.m. by his grandma, who had come to celebrate Jay's brother Greg's third birthday. Jay and his grandmother went and got doughnuts. When they got back, Jay was behaving awfully! Not minding, talking mouthy, and acting sassy by giving me dirty looks.

About an hour before his grandma intended to leave, Jay decided to get into her car. Apparently he thought if he stayed in her car, she would leave with him, and no one would realize he was gone. Of course, we realized he was in the car immediately. His grandmother and I tried to coax him out of the car for thirty minutes; he kept hiding by putting the seats down and throwing tantrums. When his grandmother left, Jay ran upstairs and had another tantrum, kicking the walls and floor. This continued for about forty-five minutes.

When Jay came downstairs after he had calmed down, I told him we were going to have dinner as a family and watch a movie in honor of his brother's birthday. When I asked Gregory what he wanted for dinner and what movie he wanted to watch, Jay had a fit because he wanted to choose. I explained to him that it was Greg's birthday and Greg's choice. Jay continued to be upset about not being able to choose what movie to watch, but he ate dinner and went upstairs and went to bed.

October 1, 2009

We had an awful morning. Jay would not mind. I took Jay's Nintendo DS away. After I took Jay to school, I had to lock myself in the bedroom and just cry because he had been acting so badly. I had the hardest time trying to control his behaviors this morning.

After I picked him up from school, I had to take him to the dentist. He was very well behaved, thank goodness. When we got home from the dentist, he did not want to go to soccer practice, but I told him it was his responsibility, because he was signed up and part of a team, and the team depended on him.

After soccer practice, we came home and ate dinner. After the kids' bath, Jay and Zack (Jay's younger brother) immediately started fighting over toy cars. I walked upstairs with a laundry basket, picked up every toy car I could find, and threw it into the basket. By this time, it was 8:00 p.m., and the kids were all supposed to be in bed, but Jay was too busy trying to find the cars to go to sleep. Jay kept breaking the lock on my bedroom door, obsessing over finding the cars and trashing my bedroom and closet in the process. Finally, at 10:00 p.m., after I escorted him to his room over and over again, he is asleep.

Meltdowns are often part of being a child, but at the young age of nine, Jay's meltdowns started turning into unstoppable episodes. The first of these episodes happened while I was driving. Jay was in the backseat, along with his two younger brothers. Jay said he wanted his window down, and I rolled it down, but only part of the way, explaining to him that it was getting chilly out and there was no need for his window to be rolled down all of the way. Jay immediately got angry and grabbed hold of the window. He began pushing and pulling at the glass, trying to manually put it down. When he discovered he was unable to do so, he threatened that if I didn't roll his window down, he would throw the car into park while I was driving. I was not going to let a nine-year-old take advantage of me; I did firmly command him to stay buckled in his seat and tell him how dangerous his verbal threats were, but he continued to kick and punch the back of the passenger seat.

When we got home about five minutes later, he was still upset but drained from his episode.

These meltdowns usually subside as quickly as they come on. Sometimes one of his meltdowns can last anywhere from about seven minutes to an hour or sometimes even longer. Part of Jay's diagnosis: Jay fell on the autism spectrum. While he is involved in his meltdown, he does not realize what he is doing or why. This is the scariest part of his disorder, in my opinion.

Jay became violent toward me, and after each incident, he did not have any recollection of the occurrence. He has said these episodes made him feel like he was unable to control his actions.

One particular morning, Jay's little brother was looking at one of Jay's magazines. When Jay saw what his brother was doing, he became furious. Jay immediately wanted to take back what was his. When I told Jay that his little brother had asked me permission to be able to look at the magazine, and that I had told him yes, Jay didn't care. He was still very upset, trying to get to his brother, chasing him around the dining-room table and through the house—whatever it took to take the magazine back. This episode went on for a good ten minutes. Jay did calm down, but when he is manic, it takes all of my energy to try to turn the situation around.

Chapter 4

Therapy

Doctors told me repeatedly that medications are most effective with therapy. Many child psychologists use play therapy to help a child open up to them. By bonding with the children, psychologists can make them feel more comfortable and become better able to help them. When I decided to seek out a therapist for Jay, I felt it was important for him to have open communication with his psychiatrist. Communication was a must, because if the psychologist feels that the child's behaviors and actions are not responding well to the prescribed medications, the parents can collaborate with the psychiatrist. I had been told that children have a tendency to metabolize psychiatric medications quickly. Over the past few years, this had become increasingly frustrating.

Since starting on medication at six years old, Jay had been on over twenty prescriptions. For the first few years, when Jay would start a new medication, it would work really well for several months, but out of the blue, he would have more meltdowns, as well as anger and emotional breakdowns.

Family therapy is very important, especially when children are involved. For this therapy, every member of the family should be present. The professional counselor helps each member of the family by teaching him or her how to interact with one another in a productive manner. A few months back, I received a call from a counselor who worked for the city; she had already met my son at school for a group counseling meet called "friendship group," which helps to improve one's social skills. The woman who runs the group asked if I would meet her once a week. This would help her understand Jay better. As an outsider looking in, she would be able to offer objective advice on discipline, family activities, communication, or whatever she thought might be beneficial to Jay as well as to our family.

Nowadays, during school, kids who have similar emotional or behavioral issues are offered group therapy up until the time they enter treatment in a residential or outpatient facility. A very positive trait has been observed among kids in a residential hospital: they can relate to one another. Kids don't generally feel comfortable alone, as they feel isolated and unable to control their behaviors. In contrast, kids in a residential hospital help one another by offering mutual support.

Behavioral therapy is a technique for replacing negative behaviors with new learned positive behaviors. E. B. Skinner was a behavioral therapist who used rewards, along with positive reinforcement, to help enforce good behaviors and associate bad behaviors with punishment.

Chapter 5

Determined to Find a Diagnosis

When I had to have my baby admitted to a hospital, my heart felt as if it were being ripped out of my chest, but I knew it was something I had to do to help him.

Once again, Jay was on new medication. On that particular day, we had gone to his therapist, as on any other Monday. This time Jay had been having meltdowns from which he just couldn't break out. Just after walking out of the door of his therapist's office, Jay, still very upset, climbed onto the second-floor edge and told me he wanted to jump off and kill himself! This scared me as nothing had ever scared me before. Once I had talked him off the ledge safely, I got him into the car and told him that I was sorry. I explained that his actions had been so extreme that I needed to find someone who could help him. I took him home and packed a bag for him, and we drove to the hospital, where they admitted him right away.

The doctors said that Jay had had an allergic reaction to the medication he was on (lithium). They were able to taper off his prescription to a safe dose for his body. Once the doctors had evaluated Jay's condition and his behavior, they started him on a new medication.

These medications worked for a few months, but after that, Jay would again struggle with meltdowns. After Jay repeated his hospital stay and tried another new set of medications, the hospital informed me there was nothing more they could do to help him, so they referred us to several residential centers for me to choose from.

I had the choice of two different medical centers: one in Arizona and the other in Texas. Living in California, I immediately wanted to go with the treatment center in Arizona, because I wanted my baby as close to home as could be, but after doing research on both hospitals, I decided the center in Texas (Meridell) could do more for us than the center in Arizona, so our baby had a bed waiting for him within two weeks.

My son had never been on a flight before leaving for his journey to the hospital in Texas. He was nervous to begin with, but when the wheels of the plane hit the runway, Jay screamed out at the top of his lungs, "We didn't die!" He sure does crack me up sometimes.

When we arrived at the facility, we saw that it was a peaceful, open ranch surrounded by trees. Jay was excited when he discovered that the hospital had cats that roamed the grounds. All the kids looked very happy, which comforted me a little. When you're considering a residential treatment center for your child, you need to understand that leaving them will be the hardest part.

The doctors took time understand each child and study his or her behaviors. They even had the ability to pinpoint the area of the brain showing a chemical imbalance. The doctors could then determine which medication would be most likely to help each child. The parents were to have family therapy sessions with their children once a week via teleconference, and once a month, they were to be there in person.

The hospital made all arrangements and paid for all flights and accommodations. After the first family visit, the child could go off grounds for overnighters with their parents. The kids spent much of the day outside playing and enjoying three-course meals three times a day; I expected to bring home a linebacker.

After about a month, we finally got the answers we'd been searching for. Jay suffers from bipolar disorder with ADHD. The testing also showed that he falls on the autism spectrum.

Leaving my nine-year-old little boy in another state for several months was the hardest decision I have ever had to make as a mom, but when I brought home my ten-year-old son, I knew it was had been the right decision and well worth it. It has been almost three years now since Jay has come home from the residential center and has been on the same medication ever since. Jay's behavior has improved immensely.

Jay had his tenth birthday in the residential treatment facility. I flew down for his birthday and brought him a cake and a couple of small presents. One present he really enjoyed was a stuffed animal that sang "Happy Birthday," and all of his family and friends back at home wrote a message on it. Jay said he slept with it and it made him less homesick.

October 28, 2008: the day we left Texas after Jay's treatment was finished.

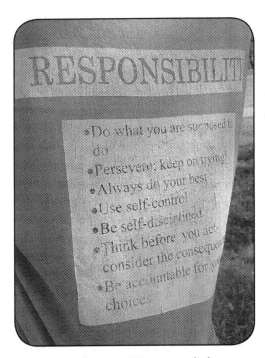

I thought this shirt was fitting. We posted these sentences on the wall once he came home, so he would remember.

➢ Do what you are supposed to do.

➢ Persevere; keep on trying!

➢ Always do your best.

➢ Use self-control.

➢ Be self-disciplined.

➢ Think before you act.

➢ Consider the consequences.

➢ Be accountable for your choices.

Jay's stay in Texas was necessary. It is important for parents to know how serious psychiatric medications are. When Jay first arrived in Texas, he went through a med wash. A med wash is when a doctor is assigned to a patient's case and decides discontinue all medications. New medications will be based upon the doctor's evaluation. The doctor and other hospital staff will then carefully observe each behavior and symptom the child expresses. When children are placed on medications, their bodies metabolize it much more quickly than an adult body, which is why the child's medications will seem to work for a while and then just stop working.

Jay's dad is an active-duty member of the military, and during Jay's stay at the treatment center in Texas, he was deployed. Months prior to Jay's stay, a family trip to Hawaii had been planned for his dad's homecoming. When it came time for our trip, I felt it was an important part of Jay's recovery to be part of family trip and to meet his dad in Hawaii after his father had been gone for six months. I spoke to both Jay's psychologists and his psychiatrist, and they agreed that missing out on a family trip could be more harmful than two more weeks of observation.

Chapter 6

Medications

Jay has had many medication changes over the years, but since his residential stay in Texas two years ago, he has remained on the same four medications. The current medications are Concerta, Seroquel, Trileptal, and Amantadine.

We've tried many medications, including the following.

Adderall, Ritalin, Strattera, and Concerta are all stimulants used to treat the symptoms of ADD and ADHD, such as hyperactivity and impulse control. Jay has tried each one of these drugs over the last seven years, but we have found that Concerta has been the most successful. Jay takes Concerta to help him focus and concentrate in school.

Jay was on Trazodone for several years to treat his depression symptoms. This medication made Jay feel sleepy, so he took it at night. Risperdal, Seroquel, Abilify, and Depakote are all used to treat bipolar as well as other disorders. Jay's reaction to Depakote was violent and agitated, and he became increasingly moody.

Over the last few years, Jay has also tried Trileptal, Wellbutrin, Amantadine, and lithium. Trileptal is used to treat seizures. Wellbutrin is an antidepressant. Amantadine is used to treat Parkinson's disease and many other conditions. Amantadine is still working well with Jay's body, even after three years. Lithium is used for a number of symptoms, including depression, anger, and mania. Lithium was the last medication we tried before Jay went to the residential treatment center in Texas. Soon after Jay began taking lithium, he started experiencing suicidal thoughts.

These are only some of the medications that you and your doctor may consider using to treat your specific disorder. Many medications are used together to help treat the disorder more effectively. You should only begin taking medications prescribed by a doctor. A person should not try to diagnose or medicate himself or herself. As always, if there is a chance of overdose, contact your poison-control center or call 911.

While writing, I have focused on Jay's manic actions. My understanding of each of his problems, along with how I have helped him to cope with his bipolar disorder, will help others in similar situations. But Jay is so much more than a bipolar child; he is my world. I don't remember life before him, and I can't picture life without him. Jay is such a funny little boy—so incredibly kind and silly. Jay has so much love in his heart, and you can feel it through his embraces. Jay can make anyone melt. I was so worried about how Jay would be when his little brothers were born, but I have to say he is the best big brother I have ever seen. Jay is protective and helpful, and he plays very well with his brothers. He is truly a precious gift from God.

Jay loves being on the surf team for his school

Chapter 7

Resources

One resource that really helped Jay was our daily emotions chart. Each day before bedtime, Jay would circle the face that he felt most closely depicted how he felt. If he was happy, he would circle the smiling face, and if he was sad, he would circle the frowning face. On the same sheet of paper, he would have to write three reasons why he was feeling the way he was.

We also used an emotions thermometer. Jay can easily look at the multicolored thermometer and express if he was in the green, happy or relaxed; yellow, a little happy; orange, a little mad; or red, extremely angry.

Jay is a child who responds well to money, and I used this to my advantage with a behavior/chore chart. The chart had two columns: chores and behaviors. Under "chores," I would list all the necessary household chores for the week: "take out trash," "clean room," "water plants," "do homework," and so on. On the other side, I would list behaviors: "hitting your brothers," "tantrums," and so on. Jay would start with $20 in play money for the week—ten for chores and ten for behaviors—and every time he failed to do his chores or didn't follow the behaviors, he would lose a dollar. At the end of the week, however, whatever play money was still left was tallied in the behavior chart, and Jay was given that amount in real cash.

I wrote this book because I feel that any pain, suffering, or hardship we endure is for a reason. I have always been open about Jay's condition because I know we are not the only family who has gone through something like this. When I was seeing one doctor after the other, not knowing why my son acted the way he did, I wished I could have found a book that described the specific actions of a child, so that I could find help and advice about how to deal with my child. It just might have helped me have a better understanding of my child, which could result in a quicker diagnosis.

Strangers, friends, and even some family members have said that I didn't punish my son enough; I even had to hear repeatedly, "If he were my child, I would spank him!" I am an extremely emotional person, and when someone talked to me like this, I would start crying, because it made me think that I was solely responsible for Jay's behavior pattern. When others think that they could be parenting more effectively than I can, it makes me angry, because I spend every day trying to help my son to be a good, honest, and responsible person, not to mention working with several doctors to help him deal with his feelings and behaviors.

I know I am a good mother, and I would do anything in this world for my children. The truth of the matter is spanking doesn't work; if spanking worked, I would spank, but it doesn't. The feelings brought on by spanking can be aggressive and angry. If I spank Jay, he becomes aggressive. This is usually when his meltdown is the most powerful; he doesn't realize what he is doing. At the time, all he knows is that he can't stop. When this happens, I can see how he falls on the autism spectrum.

Doctors sometimes use words that laypeople are unfamiliar with; I myself have been too embarrassed at times to ask the doctor to explain in more detail what he or she is telling me. If a doctor uses the word "phobia," it means being scared. The diagnosis could be anything from a fear of heights to a fear of leaving the house.

Anxiety is likely a word that you have heard before. It refers to an uneasy feeling. I tend to feel anxious before a big event: a party, the first day of school, or the impending arrival of a guest. The symptoms I encounter are pains in my chest, trouble breathing, and trouble sitting still. My son, on the other hand, used to have separation anxiety when he was small; Jay used to think that something bad was going to happen to me when we were apart. Separation anxiety is more likely to occur in children than adults.

Mania is a common occurrence for people who have bipolar disorder. My son can go days without sleep because he feels so manic. My mom, on the other hand, a grocery-store checker who has also been diagnosed with bipolar disorder, once drove to the airport during her lunch break from work on a whim and spent all the money she had on a one-way ticket to Paris, not knowing how she would afford necessities when she arrived in Paris or how she would return home to the United States.

Chapter 8

Conclusion

It has been three years since Jay was diagnosed with bipolar disorder and ADHD. Jay is a smart, sweet, kind, and loving child. As he has begun his teenage years, it is getting harder to distinguish between teenage rebellion and the symptoms of his disorder. Jay has always been an impulsive child; while the medications have decreased his dangerous behaviors, he still tends to act without thinking. It is a constant worry that he will charge into the street without looking or take something from the store without paying for it.

Stealing and lying are new issues we've been dealing with over the last year. The more time goes by, the more Jay realizes that he won't get away with negative behaviors just because he has a mental disorder. He understands that he gets punished for the negative decisions he makes, just as any other child would.

We have had good results using positive reinforcement and punishment. The type of positive reinforcement we use is the token system. We use poker chips as the tokens, but many objects can be used for the same purpose. In order for Jay to earn one token, he must show behaviors that I believe to be desirable behaviors. Once Jay earns twenty tokens, he receives a prize. Earning twenty tokens usually takes Jay about one week. The prize is something that we have decided upon prior to Jay receiving his first token; it can be anything from a candy bar to a movie to an extra hour of video-game time. Positive reinforcement shows Jay that his actions earn him rewards. Because he enjoys the rewards, Jay tries to do what is expected of him most of the time.

Punishments are also a large factor in Jay's life. When Jay does something wrong, it is understood that he is going to lose privileges. An example of this is if Jay is caught on the computer after bedtime, this action results in a loss of computer privileges. If he takes off too far on his bike, he loses the privileges of riding his bike. I try to fit the punishment with the crime. The length of time he is restricted is usually about three days, but it really depends on the extremity of his negative behaviors. Punishment teaches Jay what is acceptable and what is not by associating a wrong action with an unpleasant consequence. If you decide to work with a therapist, it is possible they will teach you how to use behavior therapy to receive more desired behaviors from your child.

The tool that I have found to work the best on Jay is positive praise. Each time he does something positive, no matter how small the action, I tell him how proud of him I am. It is important for him to know how proud of him I am, and the more I praise him, the better he usually does.

Jay's medications work well with his body chemistry. Finding the right type and dosage of medication for a child with bipolar disorder can be like "pulling the handle on a slot machine over and over again, hoping for the magical combination". It takes time and patience, but it is important that we as parents don't give up. If you keep looking, eventually you'll find it.

Disclaimer: This information should not be considered medical advice and cannot serve as a substitute for the judgment of a competent psychiatrist.

Appendix

Helpful Resources

Bloom, A., D. Schaler, J. Haeckel, J. Duff, and C. Sullivan. "Welcome to Bipolar World." Accessed in 2010. http://www. bipolarworld.net/Community/webchat.html

Lawlis, F. *The ADD Answer.* New York:

Penguin Group, 2004.

Papolos, D., and J. Papolos. *The Bipolar Child.* New York:

Broadway Books, 1999.

Scott Brunson, T. Personal blog. http://bipolarlilpeople.wordpress.com

Segal, J., and M. Smith. "Helping a Loved One with Bipolar Disorder" Accessed in 2011. http://helpguide.org/mental/bipolar_disorder_family_friends_su pport.htm

American Association of Poison Control Centers. http://www.aapcc.org/

http://www.drugs.com. Drug information site.

Meridell Achievement Center. http://www.meridell.com/

RxList, an online drug index. http://www.rxlist.com

WebMD, a source of medical information. http://www.webmd.com